BAROQUE ART
IN ITALY

by Eric Van Schaack

Department of Fine Arts
Goucher College

McGRAW-HILL BOOK COMPANY

New York   Toronto   London

BAROQUE ART IN ITALY

Like the adjective Gothic, Baroque was first used as a term of
disparagement, a synonym for the strange, the capriciously con-
trived or the bizarre. This derogatory meaning has now been
abandoned and the word Baroque is most commonly used to
define one historic period, beginning about 1600 in Italy and
lasting until about 1725. It is this period that is known as the
"Age of the Baroque." No single artistic style, however, can
encompass the astonishingly varied developments of Italian art
during this era. Changes in taste, patronage and critical theory
brought about not the gradual evolution of a single "Baroque
style" but a succession of styles. The proximity of artists of
radically differing outlooks is one of the salient features of the
period. To understand this, it is enough to realize that Andrea
Sacchi's *The Vision of St. Romuald* and Pietro da Cortona's
ceiling fresco in the Gran Salone of the Palazzo Barberini were
done by artists of almost the same age, in the same city, at very
nearly the same time (Color slides 10 and 12).

The art of Sacchi and Pietro da Cortona epitomize
the main artistic trends of the century: the classical and the
Baroque. The classical current drew its inspiration from the
masters of the High Renaissance, above all from Raphael (1483-
1520). In the *School of Athens* in the Papal Apartments of the

Vatican, Raphael had created one of the most triumphant moments of High Renaissance classicism. The clarity of organization, the simplicity of gesture, and the unity of composition with well organized groups of figures woven into a coherent pattern were all admired by the classicizing artists of the seventeenth century as being without equal. It was to this moment that they returned. And like Raphael himself, they assiduously studied the remnants of ancient statuary with which Rome abounded.

The counter trend, that of the Baroque, had its roots in the north of Italy. Where the classicizing artists turned to Raphael, the Baroque artists turned to the late Venetian masters: to Titian, Tintoretto and to Veronese as well as to the art of Correggio as seen in the frescoes in the cupolas of S. Giovanni Evangelista and the Cathedral of Parma. The dynamic movement and rich full-bodied colors of the Baroque artists of the seventeenth century were matched by their interest in compositional patterns that zig-zag back and forth within the imaginary space of the painting. Instead of the calm and restraint that marked the classicizing artists, Baroque artists preferred the excited, the agitated; wild swirls of drapery that seem to have a life of their own and saints and martyrs whose faces glow with the enthusiasm of ecstatic religious experience. Though the Baroque trend dominated and gave its name to the age, it is the ebb and flow of these two currents that give the Italian seventeenth century its richness and diversity.

For three-quarters of the century Rome was the artistic capital of Europe. Though there were flourishing local schools of painting at Venice, Bologna, Genoa, and Naples, their importance is secondary when compared to that of Rome. Artists flocked to the city, drawn by the lure of the lavish patronage of the great papal families: the Aldobrandini, the Borghese, the Barberini, the Pamphili and the Chigi, to name only an important few. But it was a group of artists who arrived in Rome in the last years of the sixteenth century that gave the impetus to artistic developments in the city and who established its commanding position.

During the final decades of the sixteenth century, there was a growing reaction against the various types of the anticlassical, complex and ambiguous style known as Mannerism. In Bologna three artists, Ludovico Carracci and his cousins Annibale and Agostino, dominated the artistic life. Working sometimes singly and sometimes as a team (when asked about their respective shares in a fresco commission, they are said to have replied "all of us did it"), the Carracci carried out a series of works of revolutionary importance. Though Ludovico was the oldest of the group, Annibale was the strongest talent, and the

Figure 1. Annibale Carracci: Caryatids and Decorative Figures (Gallery). Palazzo Farnese, Rome

fame of the Carracci's Bolognese work resulted in Annibale's summons to Rome in the mid-1590's to fresco the Gallery of the Palazzo Farnese (Color slide 1 and Figure 1). Completed shortly after 1600, the Palazzo Farnese frescoes inaugurated a new era in Italian art and contained within them the seeds of both the Baroque and classicizing trends of the century.

While Annibale Carracci was engaged on the Palazzo Farnese frescoes, another artist from Northern Italy was rising to prominence in the city. His name was Michelangelo Merisi, called Caravaggio from the place of his birth not far from Bergamo. Much remains to be discovered about Caravaggio's early career. He was born in 1573 and after some training in Milan arrived in Rome in the late 1580's. Caravaggio was ill-tempered, surly and truculent. His Roman years were punctuated by repeated brushes with the law, and much of our information about him comes from the records of the police courts. In 1606 he was accused of murdering a young man in a pitched battle following a disputed sporting contest and he fled the city. Four years later, after having wandered from Naples to Malta, Syracuse and Messina, he died of malaria.

During his early Roman years, Caravaggio had produced a number of half-figure pieces of which *The Fortune Teller* in the Louvre is one of the finest examples (Color slide 2). Caravaggio—whose modesty was never one of his strong points —undoubtedly helped to spread the story that these paintings were unflinchingly naturalistic, an unvarnished view of the world about him. In reality, however, they belong to a long tradition, especially strong in the North of Europe, and Caravaggio must be regarded as an adapter not an innovator in this field of anecdotal genre painting.

But if Caravaggio had never turned his hand to devotional painting, his fame, or infamy, would hardly have survived. Large scale frescoes and altarpieces had always been the fields in which Italian painters earned their greatest renown. Though

Figure 2. Caravaggio: David with the Head of Goliath. Borghese Gallery, Rome

Figure 3. Orazio Gentileschi: David. Palazzo Spada, Rome

an artist might engage himself creditably in other tasks, his reputation in the "official" art world—that is, the world of ecclesiastical patronage—depended upon his performance in these two areas. Caravaggio never worked in fresco. His altarpieces, though, created a sensation. Several of them, like *The Death of The Virgin* (Color slide 3), were rejected by those who had commissioned them on ground of impropriety. Caravaggio's conception of religious imagery outraged conservative religious taste and the widely circulated tale that he had called in a gypsy girl to serve as a model for *The Fortune Teller* was twisted to suggest that a drowned prostitute had been the model for the Virgin. *The Death of The Virgin* was the climax of Caravaggio's Roman career and the finest of a series of altarpieces which he painted for Roman churches from about 1597 onwards. It is in these altarpieces that Caravaggio reveals himself as a great religious painter. In the mysterious semi-darkness, the figures are lighted by a powerful illumination which accentuates the solidity of the forms. These dramatic contrasts of light and shade were the most revolutionary features of Caravaggio's late Roman manner. Even his smaller works take on the same half-lighted tone. The *David with the Head of Goliath* (Figure 2) was done for Scipione Borghese, nephew of Pope Paul V, only shortly before *The Death of The Virgin*. It was reported, probably correctly, that in the open-mouthed, wildly staring head of Goliath, Caravaggio painted his own self-portrait.

Caravaggio left Rome for good in 1606 and Annibale Carracci died in 1609. The next decade saw the artists in Rome gravitating toward one or the other of these influential figures. Those who followed in Annibale's wake were mostly artists who had been trained in the Carracci circle in Bologna. They had come to Rome to share their teacher's success and all of them were first-class fresco painters. Caravaggio, on the other hand, never had and apparently never wanted any pupils working directly with him. None of the artists whom he influenced grasped the essence of his profoundly moving religious style, but the impact of his dark manner and so-called naturalism was felt by artists of varying ages and backgrounds.

Some, like Ludovico Cardi, called "il Cigoli," (his native city) had begun their artistic training before Caravaggio was even born. A Florentine, Cigoli's anti-Mannerist style of the late sixteenth century is a counterpart of the Bolognese work of the Carracci, but after his arrival in Rome about 1604, his work took on many of the superficial aspects of Caravaggio's style. The grotesquely dressed jailers and the dark background of his *Ecce Homo* (Color slide 4) depend heavily upon Caravaggio's work.

There is little consistency among Caravaggio's followers and imitators. When Orazio Gentileschi (1563-1638) painted his *David with the Head of Goliath* (Figure 3), he was obviously

attempting to emulate Caravaggio's painting of the same subject, but Gentileschi's work still preserves the smooth modeling and the tonalities of his Florentine background. Like so many of the Caravaggesques, Gentileschi's "Caravaggio phase" is a brief one. After his arrival in England in 1626 to serve Charles I, he moved toward the art of Rubens and Van Dyck.

Carlo Saraceni's Caravaggesque phase climaxed his brief career. It was only toward the end of his stay in Rome that he produced a fine series of altarpieces in which the influence of Caravaggio can be seen growing ever stronger. *The Miracle of Saint Benno* of 1618 is the most powerful of the group (Color slide 5). Shortly after it was completed, Saraceni left Rome and went to Venice where he died in 1620.

Many of the Caravaggesque artists, in fact, returned home about this time and their later work often shows little or nothing of Caravaggio's influence. It was in the field of genre painting that Caravaggio's art had its longest survival in Italy, particularly among the group of Northern artists known as the *Bamboc-*

cianti. As we shall see, though, their cabinet pictures of everyday life had little part in the world of "official art."

The first two decades of the century were dominated not by the Caravaggesques, but by the followers of Annibale Carracci. Unlike those who tried to adapt themselves to Caravaggio's manner, the members of the Carracci circle were united by aim and training, and under Pope Gregory V Borghese (1605-21) they received the majority of the most important artistic commissions. The last years of Annibale's life had been clouded by illness, and his pupils often completed the commissions that he had begun. For the Aldobrandini family, Annibale had agreed to execute a series of painted lunettes of which only one, the lovely *Flight into Egypt* (Figure 4), was completed by him. The other five were finished by various members of the studio. Annibale was a master of landscape painting and in the later work of his pupils we find some of the finest early seventeenth century examples of this art.

Guido Reni was the oldest of the Carracci group. He had

arrived in Rome not long after 1600 and his entrance into the circle of Scipione Borghese secured for him one important commission after another, climaxed by his famous *Aurora* in the Casino dell' Aurora of the Palazzo Rospigliosi-Pallavicini (Figure 5). Like the mythological scenes in the Farnese Gallery, the *Aurora* is represented as a framed easel painting transferred to the ceiling. The cool colors and the careful organization of the figures in frieze-like fashion are characteristic of Reni's classicist orientation and the *Aurora* is the acknowledged masterpiece of this early phase of seventeenth century classicism. Reni's abrupt and still unexplained return to Bologna in 1614 at the height of his fame put an end to his commanding position in the Roman art world, but until his death in 1642 he remained one of the most important painters of the century.

Domenico Zampieri, called Domenichino, had been actively engaged with Annibale Carracci in the first years of the century. Unlike Reni, he remained in Rome almost thirty years before moving to Naples. Domenichino's paintings and frescoes have a subtle refinement of color which has always endeared them to the adherents of classical doctrine. In 1618 he painted the *Hunt of Diana* (Figure 6) for Cardinal Pietro Aldobrandini which later passed into Scipione Borghese's collection. It is one of Domenichino's most splendid mythological paintings, light hearted and with a delicate refinement of modeling. His religious works are hardly less impressive. *The Last Communion of Saint Jerome* of 1614 (Color slide 7) was one of the most admired paintings of the century and Domenichino shared with Reni the continued adulation of art theorists.

The counter tendency to this early phase of seventeenth century classicism is seen in the work of two distinguished masters: Lanfranco and Guercino. Lanfranco was the older of the two. He had been trained in his native Parma and arrived in Rome steeped in the experience of Correggio's art, an experience which was reinforced by a visit to his native town between

Figure 5. Guido Reni: Aurora. Casino dell' Aurora, Palazzo Rospigliosi-Pallavicini, Rome

Figure 6.   Domenichino:
The Hunt of Diana.
Borghese Gallery, Rome

1610 and 1612 where he saw and admired the late work of Bartolomeo Schedoni (1570-1615), a master whose importance in the formation of the Baroque style is only beginning to be appreciated. With the memory of paintings like Schedoni's *Deposition* (Figure 7) fresh in his mind, Lanfranco returned to Rome where he became the arch rival of Domenichino. A painting such as *The Ecstasy of Saint Margaret of Cortona* (Color slide 8) shows Lanfranco's early Baroque style at its best, but his Roman masterpiece was the frescoed dome of S. Andrea della Valle, a monument to which no photograph can do justice. In the early 1630's Lanfranco moved to Naples where he exerted an important influence on the local school of painting.

Giovanni Francesco Barbieri, called Guercino, arrived in Rome in 1621. The last painting he executed before leaving his native Cento, near Bologna, was the *Saint William Receiving the Habit* now in the Pinacoteca in Bologna (Color slide 9). Largely self-taught, Guercino had developed a Baroque manner of astonishing boldness and color. In his Roman works the strength and colorism of his early manner is still present, but the art climate of the city exerted a debilitating influence on his artistic thinking and he forced himself toward the classical manner with generally unhappy results. When he returned to Cento in 1623 there was a decided falling off in quality. His post-Roman works never matched the forcefulness of his early manner and the later classicizing phase of his career is of limited interest.

By the 1630's the classical and the Baroque camps had been consolidated. The conflicting theoretical positions were established and throughout the decade the two styles had an uneasy coexistence. The principal proponent of the Baroque trend was Pietro da Cortona. Early in his career he had worked for the Sacchetti family but he soon came to the attention of the Barberini family—the family of Pope Urban VIII—for whom he carried out his finest work, the frescoed ceiling in the Gran

Figure 7.   Schedoni: Deposition.
    Galleria Nazionale, Parma

Figure 8.   S. Maria della Pace
(façade), Rome

Salone of the Palazzo Barberini (Color slide 10). Here is a veritable world of movement and light, but underlying the profusion of figures is a literary conception: the glorification of Pope Urban VIII Barberini. In addition to his commanding position as a painter, Cortona was one of the most inventive architects of the century and the only man of the period able to direct full scale pictorial as well as architectural undertakings like the remodeling of the church of S. Maria della Pace (Figure 8). The immediate followers of Cortona's monumental style, though, were few, for Cortona's departure from Rome to complete the frescoes in the Sala della Stufa of the Palazzo Pitti in Florence (Color slide 11) and to carry out the frescoes in the "Rooms of the Planets" left his rival Andrea Sacchi as the most important master in Rome.

Where Cortona's art depended upon the early Baroque masters such as Lanfranco, Sacchi harks back to the Carracci followers and he had been trained by one of Annibale's pupils, Francesco Albani. During most of the 1640's his position was unchallenged. *The Vision of Saint Romuald* (Color slide 12) of about 1638/39 is not only one of his most distinguished works but a key monument in the understanding of the later development of the classicist current in Roman art. Sacchi's links with the early phase of classicism are apparent in the simplicity of organization and the restrained gestures of the characters. His subtle modulations of whitish tone in the robes of the monks were regarded by his contemporaries as a *tour de force* of refinement and variation within a consciously limited color scheme. Yet, there is a prevading warmth of color which is lacking in the work of the early Bolognese like Guido Reni, an abandonment of the rather chill tones of the *Aurora*.

The pontificate of Pope Urban VIII Barberini (1623-44) saw the emergence of the Roman Baroque. He and his immediate successors, Pope Innocent X Pamphili (1644-55) and Alexander VII Chigi (1655-67), all initiated large scale artistic

16

undertakings, both ecclesiastical and for their families. The reigning figure of this period was Giovanni Lorenzo Bernini, identified more than any other artist with the age itself. Born in Naples, Bernini was in Rome with his father—a sculptor—by the time he was six or seven, and Rome always remained the center of his artistic activities. When Urban VIII ascended the papal throne in 1623 he is said to have summoned the young Bernini and said, "It is your good fortune to see Maffeo Barberini as Pope. But we are still more fortunate that the Cavaliere Bernini lives at the time of our reign." Like the artists of the High Renaissance, Bernini was willing and able to work as sculptor, architect and painter although painting seems to have been hardly more than a diversion. It was Bernini's gift for organization and direction that brought to conclusion such vast enterprises as the decoration of the chapels and pilasters of St. Peter's, begun in 1645, or the magnificent piazza which stands in front of the church (See Figures 9a, b, c). Done between 1657 and 1667, this herculean task was accomplished in spite of jealous opposition and complex liturgical and topographical demands.

Yet, like Michelangelo before him, Bernini thought of himself first and foremost as a sculptor. The fame of his religious works should not blind us to the more personal side of his art which is seen in his superb portrait sculpture. The bust of Scipione Borghese (Figure 10) is an extraordinary portrait of Bernini's first important patron, one of the most enlightened connoisseurs of his age. The sensitive feeling for texture and the almost coloristic nuances of light and shade seem to defy the demands of the material, and the warmth and texture of the piece is matched by the extraordinary sense of fleeting expression and the expectant look in the eye. It was done in the early 1630's, not long before Scipione Borghese's death in 1633.

Bernini's most revolutionary work however, was the Cornaro Chapel in S. Maria della Vittoria where he created his un-

Figure 9.   *St. Peter's Rome*
a. Interior view
b. Air view from the apse
c. St. Peter's Square

*Figure 10.   Bernini:
Bust of Scipione Borghese.
Borghese Gallery, Rome*

*Figure 11.   Bernini: Ecstasy
of St. Theresa. Cornaro Chapel,
S. Maria della Vittoria, Rome*

forgettable *Saint Theresa* (See Color slide 13 and Figure 11). To us, the spectators, the vision of the Saint is manifested in all its wonder and we are asked to participate in the miraculous experience which seems to be taking place before our very eyes. The chapel appears to be momentarily invaded by the angels accompanying the seraph who pierces the Saint's heart with the arrow of Divine Love. No other work so clearly reveals Bernini's ability to weld the arts of sculpture, architecture, and painting together to express the religious sentiment of his age.

Yet the important ecclesiastical commissions of Pietro da Cortona, Andrea Sacchi, and Bernini represent only the "official" side of the Roman art world. At the same time there was a great vogue for the genre paintings of daily life which were the specialty of the group of artists led by the Dutchman Pieter van Laer. Because of a physical deformity he was nicknamed *"Bamboccio"* (big baby) and his followers and imitators were derisively known as the *Bamboccianti*. Van Laer's *The Doughnut Seller* (Color slide 14) is an excellent example of this work. These artists, operating on the borders of the official art world, were held in contempt by artists like Sacchi whose conception of art as ennobling was diametrically opposed to the anecdotal, amusing, and often risqué works of the *Bamboccianti*. Writing to his teacher and old friend Francesco Albani in October of 1651, Sacchi complained of the decline of "serious painting" in Rome at the hands of those *Bamboccianti* who painted "a rogue hunting for lice and another drinking soup from a dish . . . or a Bacchus vomiting." "This," he wrote, "is the unhappy state of painting."

At this point we must turn our attention from Rome to the provinces. During the seventeenth century several Italian cities developed important schools of painting and if their importance is less than that of the capital, they are by no means without interest. Many masters who never or seldom visited Rome are deserving of mention.

In Venice the artists who had been trained in the sixteenth century tradition of Titian, Tintoretto, and Veronese held sway for most of the first third of the new century. What innovations developed in Venice during this period were sparked by the foreign artists who visited the city to study at first hand the masterpieces of Venetian sixteenth century painting. Two artists, the German born Johann Lys and the Roman Domenico Fetti, both of whom died young, arrived in Venice in the early 1620's. Fetti had worked for years at the Court of the Gonzagas in Mantua and created a number of small scale illustrations of Biblical parables (Color slide 15). These translations of the Biblical teachings into everyday terms are an aspect of Caravaggio's naturalism but Fetti's main contacts were probably not with Caravaggio himself but with his followers such as Carlo Saraceni. When he died in Venice in 1623, Fetti had already turned more toward lighter Venetian tones, moving away, as so many artists did, from the experience of Caravaggio. Johann Lys lived in Venice for most of the 1620's and was more successful working on a monumental scale than Fetti. His *Vision of St. Jerome* (Color slide 16) was painted for an altar in the church of S. Niccolò dei Tolentini shortly before Lys died in the terrible plague of 1629/30. According to his biographer Sandrart, Lys alternated between periods of idleness and periods of intense day and night activity in which he would seldom pause for sleep or nourishment. His passionate, personal vision and freedom of handling is a harbinger of the Venetian Rococo.

Venice was also the center of activity for the last fourteen or so years of Bernardo Strozzi's life. Even his early work in Genoa shows a richness and freedom of color which anticipates the Baroque. (Strozzi's work undoubtedly influenced the much younger Giovanni Battista Gaulli whose Gesù frescoes are, as we shall see, the finest expression of the Roman High Baroque.) Strozzi was a prolific painter, often duplicating his

Figure 12. Guido Reni:
Madonna and Saints.
Pinacoteca, Bologna

compositions with little or no variation and, unlike Fetti or Lys, much of his finest work is monumental religious painting such as the *Saint Sebastian* in S. Benedetto, Venice (Color slide 17). There is a wondrous range of color in all of Strozzi's work and later Venetian painting owed much to him.

In contrast to Venice, Bologna's importance declined as the century progressed. Reni had returned to Bologna in 1614 and established himself as the most important figure in the city. His *Madonna and Saints* (Figure 12), painted as a thank offering for the end of the plague which struck Bologna in 1630, is one of the best monumental works of his later period. Reni's position as the head of a large group of artists drew the best of the younger men into his orbit, and while there were a number of talented and attractive artists in that group, their importance is only local.

It was in the field of decorative architectural painting that the Bolognese artists continued to hold a dominant place. Angelo Michele Colonna (1600-87) and Agostino Mitelli (1609-60) worked together in Rome, Genoa, Parma, Madrid and Florence creating a style of work in which astonishingly illusionistic architectural representation is combined with figure groups to give the impression of a spacious interior. The rooms which they decorated in the Palazzo Pitti in Florence, now the Museo degli Argenti, are a fine example of their combined efforts (Figure 13).

In Lombardy, Milan had been the artistic center until the end of the third decade, but for the latter part of the century the most interesting developments were to be seen in Bergamo and Brescia. Bergamo particularly deserves mention for the fine portrait painters and painters of still lifes who were active there. Among the latter group, Evaristo Baschenis is supreme. To this day, much of his career is still shrouded in mystery but his representations of musical instruments are among the finest still lifes done during the century and some of them, like the splendid example in Brussels, are worthy to be classed among

Figure 13.
Angelo Michele Colonna
and Agostino Mitelli: Interior,
Palazzo Pitti, Florence

the best in the long history of Italian art (Color slide 18).

Roman art of the second half of the century presents a complex artistic situation with a variety of artistic tendencies. On one hand there were the imaginative, romantic productions of Salvator Rosa. An etcher as well as a painter, Rosa was also a poet, actor, musician and self-appointed critic of manners and taste. His few religious paintings have a curiously bizarre quality which sets them off from the broad currents of mid-century taste and one can see the appeal that they had for the nineteenth century Romantics (Color slide 19). He and a few other artists form a group unto themselves and in many of them, such as

Rosa, artist and politician are combined. Rosa's antagonism to all vested interests did not exclude the great Bernini himself and in 1639 Rosa presented a theatrical production whose prologue contained a violent satire against Bernini's theatrical ventures. The furor which this aroused made it expedient for Rosa to leave Rome and retire to Florence where he set himself up as the leading figure of a group of literary and artistic personalities.

By the time Rosa returned to Rome in the early 1670's, one of Bernini's collaborators had received the most important commission of the day. This was the Genoese painter Giovanni Battista Gaulli (called Baciccio) whose work in the Gesù is one of the most magnificent monuments of Baroque Rome (Color slide 20). Like so many of the finest talents of seventeenth century Genoa, Gaulli had sought his fortune outside of his native city. In the formation of his vivid, coloristic style, the work of Bernardo Strozzi was of key importance but later figures, such as Giovanni Benedetto Castiglione, also played a part.

Figure 14.
Gaulli: Gesù ceiling (details).
Gesù, Rome

Figure 15.   Caracciolo:
St. Peter Liberated from Prison.
Church of the Misericord, Naples

Castiglione's *Crucifixion* (See color slide 21) reveals his intensively personal manner at its finest and the knowledge of Castiglione's Genoese works played an important part in the development of Gaulli's dramatic style. Gaulli's collaboration with Bernini, though, was decisive in the development of his artistic vision and the ceiling frescoes of the Gesù in Rome represent an extension of revolutionary ideas. As in the *Saint Theresa*, the limits of painting, sculpture and architecture have been broken in the Gesù ceiling and all three have been combined to give an overwhelmingly dramatic effect (Figure 14).

The Gesù ceiling marked the height of the Roman Baroque. Henceforth the dominating factor was to be the late phase of classicism as typified by Carlo Maratti, an artist who by the time he died was regarded as the most important talent of his day. As a pupil of Andrea Sacchi, Maratti represents the heir to a long tradition. He was a splendid portrait painter, one of the best of the century, but his monumental altarpieces, such as *The Virgin Appearing to Saint Philip Neri* (Color slide 22), are perhaps his finest works.

Maratti's long career saw the climax of Rome's importance in the seventeenth century. For the concluding act of the "Age of the Baroque" we must turn to Naples. During the first half of the seventeenth century, Naples had been a fertile and productive center of the arts. Caravaggio's visit to the city in 1606-7 had left in its wake an important group of painters, all of whom, in varying ways, responded to the dramatic eloquence of his late manner. Even the best of them, though, such as Giovanni Battista Caracciolo (died 1637) or the Spaniard Jusepe Ribera (1591-1652) moved away from Caravaggio under the impact of the Bolognese artists, particularly Lanfranco who had settled in the city from 1634 until 1646. The social agitation against the often oppressive rule of the Spanish Viceroys, climaxed by the ill-fated riots led by a young fish-seller known as Masaniello in 1647, alienated some of the artists from their native city. But

thologies which are the most popular of Solimena's works. Solimena's academy in Naples was enormously influential and even artists of the older generation flocked to him. Today the churches in and around Naples are still filled with their work. Little of it rises above mediocrity, but nevertheless it is stamped with the unmistakable mark of the master's grand manner.

Solimena's art is a connecting link between the seventeenth and eighteenth centuries. When he died in 1747 at the age of ninety, Venice had already become the most important art center of the day and in Venice it was Tiepolo, Canaletto, and Guardi who were to become the masters of the Italian Rococo. Rome's domination of the arts had become a thing of the past and the Age of the Baroque was ended.

· 1 ·

ANNIBALE CARRACCI
(1560-1609)
The Gallery
Fresco
Palazzo Farnese, Rome

In 1595 Annibale Carracci was called to Rome from his native Bologna by Cardinal Prince Odoardo Farnese to decorate some of the rooms in the family palace. After completing the so-called *Camerino* about 1597, he turned his attention to the Gallery which was destined to house some of the classical marbles from the Farnese family's rich collection. With the help of his brother Agostino, Annibale completed most of the ceiling decoration of the Gallery by 1600. The walls above the entrance door and at the end of the Gallery were finished three or four years later and for this phase of the decoration Annibale had the help of some of the younger Bolognese artists, among them Domenichino.

The power of Love, symbolized by episodes from Classical mythology (many of them from the *Metamorphoses* of Ovid), is the dominant theme of the Gallery. The principal scenes are represented as simulated easel paintings which have been raised to the ceiling and set against an illusionistic architectural framework, flanked by painted medallions and life-like figures of youths. Although this system of ceiling decoration, as opposed to completely illusionistic representations, had few imitators, Annibale's work nevertheless represented a turning point in the history of Italian monumental painting. What he accomplished was no less than a revitalization of the classical heritage as represented by antique art and Raphael, an achievement which was fully understood and appreciated by his contemporaries.

By his return to the traditional sources, plus his re-establishment of the High Renaissance working procedure in which every step of the undertaking was preceeded by numerous preparatory drawings, Annibale created a monument which became a fountainhead for the classicizing tendencies of the seventeenth century. In addition, his vibrant color scheme acted as an impetus for the coloristic developments which found their full flowering in the High Baroque. For over two hundred years, the Farnese Gallery was ranked along with Michelangelo's Sistine Ceiling and Raphael's Vatican *Stanze* as one of the key monuments in the history of European art.

CARAVAGGIO
(1573-1610)
The Fortune Teller
Canvas, 39″ x 52″
Louvre, Paris

The classically minded art theorist and critic Giovanni Pietro Bellori wrote in 1672 that the young Caravaggio, disdaining those hallowed canons of good art, ancient statuary and the paintings and frescoes of Raphael, declared that "Nature alone was to serve as the object of his brush." To prove his point, Bellori continues, Caravaggio brought in a young gypsy girl from the street and used her as a model for his painting of a young man having his fortune told "and in these two half-length figures, Caravaggio rendered Nature so plainly that he succeeded in making good his words." This painting is almost certainly the one cited by Bellori. Caravaggio painted it about 1594, not long after he arrived in Rome. In 1665, it was sent to Paris as a gift from Prince Camillo Pamphili to Louis XIV.

The story of Caravaggio's "faithfulness to nature" took deep root in the seventeenth century art world. His half-length figure pieces were often imitated by northern artists as well as Italian ones and enjoyed a great popularity. The legend, though, is hardly confirmed by Caravaggio's paintings themselves. This young dandy, in his fantastic costume with puffed-up sleeves and feathered hat, is more like a parody of Giorgione's warriors than a realistic representation of late sixteenth century Roman costume. Rather than a slice of life, it is an anecdotal representation of the encounter between an over-dressed, somewhat naïve young man and a street girl whose winning smile is probably the first step in getting her hands on his purse. It harks back, in fact, to a northern tradition of genre painting. Popular as they were, Caravaggio's genre paintings were less influential than his religious paintings like *The Death of The Virgin* (Color slide 3) which outraged the conservative religious taste of the day and marked the beginning of a new era in Italian art.

· 3 ·

CARAVAGGIO
(1573-1610)
The Death of The Virgin
Canvas, 145″ x 96½″
Louvre, Paris

Caravaggio's *The Death of The Virgin* was the last major work of his turbulent Roman years and a climax of his artistic activity in the capital. It was painted for the Discalced Carmelite church of S. Maria della Scala shortly before he fled from the city in May, 1606, but almost immediately rejected by the church after being criticized for lacking those ennobling qualities suitable to devotional painting. Discerning critics, however, realized its value. On the recommendation of Rubens, who was in the city at the time, it was purchased by the Duke of Mantua. It was sent to England when the Mantuan collections were sold in 1627 and was eventually acquired for the collection of Louis XIV of France.

Contemporary criticism of this painting—it was even suggested that Caravaggio's model for the Virgin had been a drowned prostitute—shows how disturbing Caravaggio's religious art was to conservative religious taste. Nevertheless, Caravaggio's restatement of religious themes in simplified and deeply human terms was to play an important part in the development of seventeenth century religious imagery.

But Caravaggio's style was hardly less influential than his conception of religious art and no less criticized by those who considered themselves the heirs of the classical tradition. Although he had no pupils in the true sense of the word, there were few artists during the first decades of the century who did not fall at least for a time under his influence. In spite of critical opposition, Caravaggio's work remained one of the dominant influences in Italian painting for the next century and a half.

· 4 ·

LUDOVICO CARDI
called "IL CIGOLI"
(1559-1613)
Ecce Homo
Panel, 65″ x 53″
Palazzo Pitti, Florence

In Florentine seventeenth century painting Cigoli occupies a position which corresponds to that of Annibale Carracci in Bologna. Cigoli, more than any other Florentine painter of his generation, was able to comprehend the meaning of the "artistic revolution" which had been initiated in Rome by Caravaggio and Annibale Carracci. In true Renaissance tradition, he was active as an architect and sculptor as well as a painter. From 1604 onward the center of his activities was Rome and about 1606 he painted his *Ecce Homo* representing Christ, crowned with thorns, being displayed to the crowd. Cigoli's debt to Caravaggio is striking but it is worth noting that this painting, according to Cigoli's biographer, was executed in a three-way competition in which Caravaggio himself participated. When all three paintings were completed, the patron was so satisfied with Cigoli's that he kept it for himself and gave the others away.

While Cigoli and other artists found it easy enough to adopt the dark background and heavily shadowed figures of Caravaggio's late Roman manner, they were unable to infuse their works with the sense of sincere devotion which strikes us so forcibly in Caravaggio's religious paintings. It was the superficial rather than the essential part of Caravaggio's style that they were able to capture. Still Cigoli must be counted the first important Florentine painter of the new era, one whose work marks the beginning of the seventeenth century school of painting in Florence.

35

· 5 ·

CARLO SARACENI
(1579-1620)

The Miracle of St. Benno

Canvas, 94″ x 70″

S. Maria dell' Anima, Rome

The Venetian born Carlo Saraceni arrived in Rome in the late 1590's. He soon fell under the influence of the German painter Adam Elsheimer and produced a number of fine, small-scale paintings on copper much in the Elsheimer manner. After the German artist's death in 1610, Saraceni turned to Caravaggio and became one of the most important figures among the group of painters who, in spite of their differences, can be called "the Caravaggesques." Between 1614 and 1618 Saraceni produced a series of altarpieces in which the ever growing influence of Caravaggio can be clearly traced. *The Miracle of St. Benno* is the climax of the series, one of two paintings which Saraceni executed for the Roman church of S. Maria dell' Anima. The companion piece, *The Martyrdom of St. Lambertinus,* is also still in place and Saraceni received the final payment for both paintings in 1618.

The miracle of the Saint who discovers the keys in the belly of a fish is rendered with a gravity and solemnity almost worthy of Caravaggio himself. The neutral background, dramatic lighting and unadorned characters all hark back to Caravaggio's Roman works. Caravaggio's direct influence, intense though it was, was soon to be temporarily eclipsed by the work of Annibale Carracci's followers. By the time Saraceni painted this picture, the leading artistic current in the city was the early phase of seventeenth century classicism, principally exemplified by the work of Guido Reni and Domenichino (Figure 5 and Slide 7). *The Miracle of St. Benno* was Saraceni's last important commission in Rome and he died in Venice two years later, leaving behind him some works which introduced the Caravaggesque style into the Veneto.

· 6 ·

GUIDO RENI
(1575-1642)

Cleopatra

Canvas, 48″ x 37¾″

Palazzo Pitti, Florence

Of all the younger Bolognese artists trained in the Carracci circle in Bologna, Guido Reni had the most immediate success in Rome. Yet, by 1614 he had returned to his native Bologna where he remained almost uninterruptedly until his death. As the head of a large, active studio he dominated the artistic life of the city and orders came to him from all parts of Europe. In January of 1640 the Marchese Ferdinando Cospi, Bolognese agent for the Grandy Duchy of Tuscany, sent Reni's *Cleopatra* to Prince Leopoldo de' Medici, brother of Grand Duke Ferdinando II.

Reni has represented the queen at the moment in which she has bared her breast for the serpent's lethal sting. There are no weeping attendants, none of the archaeological detail which would specifically identify the time or place. Instead of a reconstruction of an historical incident, we are given a poignantly personal drama. The Queen takes her own life in a moment of passionate intensity, transfigured by a vision which for us must remain a mystery. The pale, silvery tonality of the painting is characteristic of the final phase of Reni's artistic evolution. None of the artists of the younger generation in Bologna quite escaped his influence and echoes of his work can be seen throughout the seventeenth and eighteenth centuries.

· 7 ·

DOMENICO ZAMPIERI
called "DOMENICHINO"
(1581-1641)

*The Last Communion
of St. Jerome*

Canvas, 165″ x 100″
Vatican Gallery, Rome

In October, 1614, Domenichino's *The Last Communion of St. Jerome* (signed and dated: Dom. Zamperius Bonon. f. a. MDCXIV) was unveiled on the high altar of S. Girolamo della Carità in Rome. Because of its dependence upon a painting of the same subject by Agostino Carracci, now in the Pinacoteca, Bologna, the charge of "plagiarism" was leveled against Domenichino by his bitter rival Lanfranco who went to the trouble to circulate an engraving of Agostino's painting in order to substantiate his charge. In actuality, far from being a copy or even an adaptation, Domenichino's painting is a complete reinterpretation of the work he had known so well in his home town. Every detail has been modified in keeping with Domenichino's far more classical orientation and, in spite of Lanfranco's efforts, *The Last Communion of St. Jerome* brought Domenichino dramatically to the attention of the Roman art world.

With Reni's departure from Rome in 1614, Domenichino assumed the position of first artist in the city. *The Last Communion of St. Jerome* reveals his gift for spatial organization and skill in handling large compositions with many figures. Framed within the monumental verticality of the architecture is a delightful landscape, forerunner of the type of background Domenichino was to provide for his superb, small, cabinet pictures. It is undoubtedly Domenichino's finest religious work. Poussin considered it the equal of Raphael's *Transfiguration* and throughout the seventeenth century it was commonly acknowledged as one of the finest paintings in Rome.

· 8 ·

GIOVANNI LANFRANCO
(1582-1647)

*The Ecstasy of St. Margaret
of Cortona*

Canvas, 91″ x 73″
Palazzo Pitti, Florence

In the early 1620's Lanfranco executed this painting for an altar in the church of S. Maria Nuova in Cortona. It was later removed from the church by Prince Ferdinando de' Medici and became part of the Grand Ducal collections in Florence.

Both in its unrestricted representation of ecstatic emotion and its vivid, glowing color, Lanfranco's painting looks forward to the fully developed Baroque phase of seventeenth century painting. By comparing it with Reni's *Aurora* of a few years earlier (See Figure 5), one can see the gap which separated Lanfranco from the precursors of seventeenth century classicism. Lanfranco had begun his career in Rome in the midst of the Carracci circle, but his two year sojourn in his native Parma (1610-12) renewed his contact with the art of Correggio and acquainted him with the late work of Bartolomeo Schedoni (See Figure 7). These contacts drastically altered his outlook and pointed him toward the stronger contrasts of light and shade and the dramatic coloring which mark his style of the 1620's, the climax of which is his decoration of the dome of S. Andrea della Valle in Rome. The success of Lanfranco's work brought an end to the early phase of seventeenth century classicism and pointed the way to the developments of Pietro da Cortona. Lanfranco's concept of visionary experience can also be seen as a forerunner of Bernini's work, in particular his *St. Theresa* (See color slide 13).

GIOVANNI FRANCESCO
BARBIERI
called "GUERCINO"
(1591-1666)

St. William Receiving the Habit

Canvas, 136″ x 90½″
Pinacoteca, Bologna

Guercino's *St. William Receiving the Habit* is the last important commission he undertook before going to Rome. It was finished in 1620, destined for an altar in the church of S. Gregorio, Bologna. After having been taken to Paris by the French in 1796, it was returned to Bologna in 1816-17 and entered the gallery.

The artistic style of the young Guercino was largely formed by the work of Ludovico Carracci in Bologna and certain painters from nearby Ferrara. In the five years previous to his Roman sojourn of 1621-23, he produced a group of altarpieces in which Bolognese and Ferrarese influences have been combined with extraordinary results. One of the finest of these is the *St. William*, a work which reveals Guercino's vigorous talents at their best. The importance of Guercino's early work, and the gap which separated him from those classically oriented artists whose influence predominated in Rome during the early years of the century, can be seen by comparing Guercino's *St. William* with Reni's *Aurora* (See Figure 5). Where Reni's figures have been isolated by a clear light, Guercino's canvas is bathed in a mellow glow which seems to dissolve the individual forms. The cool tones of Reni's work are in direct opposition to the mellow colors of Guercino's palette. As opposed to the frieze-like character of Reni's composition, Guercino's figures are oriented in depth with a foreground, middle distance and background. While Reni's work is the epitome of the early classical phase of seventeenth century painting, Guercino's work already shows all those features which will become characteristic of the Baroque.

During his stay in Rome, Guercino's style began to change, largely due to the theoretical and critical speculations of the circle of which he was a part. He continued in this direction after he returned to his native Cento, bringing his work more into line with the ideals of the classical camp. His later work is somewhat of a disappointment when compared to the freer, more dynamic works of his pre-Roman and Roman years.

· 10 ·

PIETRO DA CORTONA
(1596-1669)

*The Glorification of The Reign
of Pope Urban VIII*

Fresco
Gran Salone, Palazzo Barberini,
Rome

Pietro da Cortona's ceiling fresco in the family palace of the Barberini Pope Urban VIII was one of the most important and influential undertakings of the century. Work was begun in 1633 and completed in 1639. Though it represents a synthesis of many artistic traditions, it shows above all the effects of Cortona's direct experience of Venetian painting—particularly Veronese—which he acquired during a visit to Venice while the work was in progress. During most of the time that he was occupied with the Barberini ceiling, Cortona was the President of the Academy of St. Luke, the most important artistic organization in the city, and the importance of the commission plus his authoritative position combined to make Cortona the leading figure of the decade.

The subject of the Barberini ceiling is a complex allegorical-mythological tribute to the virtues and sound policies of Pope Urban VIII. The three bees at the top of the fresco are the emblem of the Barberini family and also symbolic representations of Divine guidance and care. Surrounding them is a laurel wreath held aloft by the Muses, an allusion to Urban VIII's literary efforts. Near the center of the vault is the figure of Immortality who is about to bestow the crown of stars on the personification of Divine Providence. At the sides of the vault are scenes from classical mythology which symbolize the Pope's political and economic successes. In essence, the Pope, as the agent of Divine Providence, has successfully manifested the Divine Will and is worthy of immortality.

Within this complex literary program, however, there is not a hint of didactic pedantry. Long before our intellectual curiosity is challenged by the meaning of the work, our eye is delighted by the exuberant colors and the masterful way in which all the elements have been drawn together. The illusionistic framework of the ceiling is interpenetrated by its surrounding elements and by comparison with Annibale Carracci's Farnese ceiling (Color slide 1), we can see how the simulated ceiling paintings at the sides of Cortona's vault have expanded their borders and have been drawn into a coordinated relationship with the whole, even, as at the lower edge, destroying the framework itself. In its organization the Barberini ceiling owes much to North Italian tradition. It is the finest monument of the Baroque trend of seventeenth century painting and occupies a key place in the history of illusionistic ceiling painting.

· 11 ·

PIETRO DA CORTONA
(1596-1669)

The Age of Gold

Fresco
Sala della Stufa,
Palazzo Pitti, Florence

In the midst of his work on the Palazzo Barberini (Color slide 10), Pietro da Cortona left Rome to travel through northern Italy. He arrived in Florence late in June of 1637 and was invited by Grand Duke Ferdinando II to carry out a series of frescoes in the so-called Sala della Stufa of the Palazzo Pitti. The subject was to be a theme from Ovid's *Metamorphoses,* the "Four Ages of Man." Before Cortona left Florence in September of the same year he had completed two of the frescoes, the *Age of Gold* and the *Age of Silver.* He returned to Florence in 1640 to complete that work and to undertake the decoration of the "Rooms of the Planets" which were eventually completed by his pupil, Ciro Ferri.

The *Age of Gold* is a splendid recreation of one of mankind's most cherished dreams, the wonderous age of easy abundance and little toil. Cortona's paradise is a blessed and light-hearted world of almost innocent delight where even the lion allows himself to be bedecked with flowers by the laughing children. The brilliance and spontaneity of the execution belies the careful preparation of every stage of the work and the numerous drawings which survive testify to the care which Cortona lavished on each figure. The Sala della Stufa is undoubtedly Cortona's masterpiece in fresco, and one of the outstanding artistic accomplishments of the century.

· 12 ·

ANDREA SACCHI
(1599-1661)

The Vision of St. Romuald

Canvas, 122″ x 69″
Vatican Gallery, Rome

During the 1630's the Roman Academy of St. Luke became the scene of a controversy which was to have considerable effect on the Roman art world. Two opposing camps were formed. One, headed by Pietro da Cortona, advocated that historical paintings should be multi-figured compositions with a narrative structure which contained both a principal and secondary theme. The opposition, headed by Andrea Sacchi, maintained that the number of figures should be limited and the narrative compressed into a single, dramatic episode. A comparison between Sacchi's gravely majestic *The Vision of St. Romuald* of about 1638/39 and Pietro da Cortona's Barberini ceiling (Color slide 10) reveals the differences which separated the two theoretical positions.

Sacchi's painting was commissioned for the high altar of the Camaldolese Church in Rome. It represents St. Romuald, the late eleventh century founder of the Camaldolese Order, telling of his dream in which he saw the members of the order passing up to Heaven after their death. The visionary scene in the background explains the meaning of the discourse which holds the Saint's fellow monks enraptured, and the presentation has a solemnity and intensity which mark this painting as one of the masterpieces of the classical camp. Sacchi is one of the key figures in the classical current of Roman art. He was trained by a pupil and collaborator of Annibale Carracci, Francesco Albani. Eventually it was Sacchi's followers who dominated the Roman art scene, particularly his pupil Carlo Maratti. Maratti, in turn, became one of the chief sources for the transmission of classicism to the eighteenth century (See color slide 22).

BERNINI
(1598-1680)

The Cornaro Chapel

Fresco painting, sculpture,
and architecture
S. Maria della Vittoria, Rome

From 1645 until 1652 Bernini was engaged in the remodeling of the left transept of the church of S. Maria della Vittoria, transforming it into a sepulchral chapel for the family of Cardinal Federigo Cornaro. Since the church belonged to the Carmelite Order, it was decided to adorn the altar with a sculptured representation of St. Theresa, the Spanish founder of the Order of Discalced Carmelites. In recounting one of her mystic visions, St. Theresa wrote that an angel had appeared to her and transfixed her heart with the arrow of Divine Love. It was this moment of visionary experience that Bernini chose to represent, one which had been cited in the Saint's Bull of Canonization of 1622. The Saint swoons before the heavenly radiance of the divine messenger, who holds aloft the arrow which will unite her soul with that of Christ.

To express this moment of visionary experience and to make the beholder a part of it, Bernini daringly overstepped the traditional boundaries between painting, sculpture, and architecture. The vault of the chapel appears to be "destroyed" by the hosts of angels who invade it. The altarpiece itself seems to float magically in mid-air and to have only momentarily occupied the architectural niche. A concealed light illuminates the group and the real light mingles with the sculptured rays which stream downward. At the sides of the chapel Bernini represented the members of the Cornaro family, interrupted at their devotions, as the astonished witnesses to the scene. Like them, we seem to have before our eyes a scene which is actually taking place in the chapel.

Bernini first experimented with combining fresco and stucco work in the Cappella Pio in S. Agostino, Rome, but the Cornaro Chapel far surpasses all previous efforts in this direction. The idea that the divisions between the arts were not sacrosanct was central to Bernini's artistic thinking. It was taken up by numerous other artists, among them Giovanni Battista Gaulli in his transformation of the Gesù (See color slide 20). Eventually it spread throughout the length and breadth of Europe.

Van Laer had left his native Haarlem in 1623 and arrived in Rome two years later, in the spring of 1625. Before he returned home nineteen years later, he had become the most prominent member of a group of northern artists—mostly Dutch—whose paintings of everyday life enjoyed considerable popularity. Because of his humped back, van Laer was given the nickname of *"il Bamboccio"* (big baby) and his followers and imitators were known disparagingly as the *Bamboccianti*. Van Laer and the *Bamboccianti* had no part in the important ecclesiastical commissions of the 1630's and 1640's. Instead, they supported themselves by producing cabinet pictures of the popular life of Rome, representing street vendors, artisan's shops, peasants mourning the death of their mules, or an itinerant dentist practicing in the Piazza Navona. It was their humble subject matter that earned the *Bamboccianti* the critics censure for representing life as being "worse than it was," but criticism hardly lessened the popularity of their work. In the midst of the "official art world" of Rome, the *Bamboccianti* represent a survival of the naturalistic traditions of Caravaggio.

Even van Laer's critics, however, admitted the artistic quality of his paintings which seemed to them "like an open window." *The Doughnut Seller* is a striking "slice of life" of lower class Roman life of the 1630's and 1640's, not the Rome of magnificent ruins or ecclesiastical ceremony but the humble life of the common people, rendered with an impartiality of vision, sympathy, and a lively curiosity.

The Lost Silver is an illustration of a parable from the gospel of St. Luke (15: 8-9) which begins: "Either what woman having ten pieces of silver, if she lose one piece, doth not light a candle, and sweep the house, and seek diligently till she find it?" It is generally considered the earliest of Fetti's parable paintings and may have been done in 1618 when Fetti was in Florence at the court of Grand Duke Cosimo II, brother-in-law of Fetti's patron, Ferdinando Gonzaga, Duke of Mantua.

Fetti had entered the service of the Mantuan Dukes in 1613 as a court painter and custodian of the Ducal art collections, a position which he held until shortly before his death. During the nearly ten years that he served the court, he created a unique series of cabinet pictures illustrating the New Testament parables. Many of them exist in numerous versions, some by Fetti and some by his associates. It is very likely that many of them were used to decorate a single room in the Palazzo Ducale. Stylistically, these parable paintings owe a great deal to northern artists such as Adam Elsheimer. In the painting of *The Lost Silver* the entire composition is welded together by the dramatic light of the candle and such use of light is often seen in Elsheimer's work. Yet, though parables had often been illustrated before Fetti's time, he is unique in having made them practically his specialty.

· 16 ·

JOHANN LYS

(ca. 1597-1629/30)

The Vision of St. Jerome

Canvas, 88½" x 69"

S. Niccolò dei Tolentini, Venice

Venetian art of the first half of the seventeenth century was radically influenced by the foreign and non-Venetian artists who had visited the city. Saraceni, bringing with him the lessons learned from Caravaggio in Rome, died in Venice in 1620; Domenico Fetti died there in 1623; and in the terrible plague of 1629/30 the German born Johann Lys (or Liss) died in the city which had been his home since the early 1620's. *The Vision of St. Jerome* is one of Lys' last works, done shortly before 1628/29. It seems to be composed in a moment of intense dramatic inspiration, and is the latest—and best—of the three versions of the same subject which Lys executed.

When seen side by side with the work of Lys, the productions of native Venetian artists of the first part of the century, many of them still linked to the manner of Titian and Tintoretto, seem feeble by comparison. Though he lived only thirty-four years, Lys developed a manner of startling boldness and vigor, one which is almost a harbinger of the future greatness of eighteenth century Venetian painting and the work of Tiepolo. The extraordinary freedom of the composition, the rich texture of the pigment and the bursts of color which give such a vibrant luminosity to the painting are Lys' legacies to Venetian art.

· 17 ·

BERNARDO STROZZI

(1581-1644)

St. Sebastian

Canvas, 169" x 79"

S. Benedetto, Venice

When he was still in his teens, the Genoese Bernardo Strozzi became a Capuchin monk but after 1610 he was granted special privileges, among them the right to wear secular religious dress. In 1630, though, with the death of his dependent mother, Strozzi was faced with the prospect of having his privileges curtailed and rebelled against returning to the monastery. According to his biographer, Strozzi was placed in the prison of the monastery from whence he fled to Venice.

The *St. Sebastian* is one of Strozzi's most noted works in Venice and one of his finest religious paintings. All the principal figures have been ordered in a dynamic foreground group, almost pushing out of the picture plane toward the spectator. The brush work is free and vigorous, hardly concerned with subtle nuances of detail but aiming for an almost overpowering effect. Strozzi's art made a lasting impression, not only in his native Genoa but also in Venice where he spent the later part of his life. The Venetian painters of the late seventeenth century owed much to Strozzi and other non-Venetians like Fetti and Lys who settled in the city (See color slides 15, 16).

· 18 ·

EVARISTO BASCHENIS
(1607?-1677)

Musical Instruments

Canvas, 39″ x 57½″
Brussels, Musées Royaux
des Beaux-Arts

In Lombardy the most active center of artistic production for the first three decades of the seventeenth century had been Milan. The disastrous plague which devastated the city in 1630 (so vividly described in Manzoni's *The Betrothed*) and the death of the city's principal patron, Archbishop Federico Borromeo, in 1631 brought an end to this phase and for the rest of the century the production of Milanese artists has little more than a provincial interest. It was in Bergamo that the finest paintings in Lombardy were produced during the second half of the seventeenth century. The painters, most of them provincial artists reflecting a long tradition of naturalism that is also seen in Caravaggio's works, produced an art which was primarily concerned with the representation of the tangible world and it was the Bergamasque milieu which formed one of the finest painters of still lifes in the history of Italian art: Evaristo Baschenis.

Almost nothing is known about Baschenis except that he was a parish priest who had been trained exclusively by local men. Paintings of musical instruments were his specialty and many of the instruments represented can be identified as those which were being produced in the famous Cremona factory of the Amati family. Baschenis rendered the textures and finishes of these splendid instruments with crisp precision and loving care. There is a quality to his paintings which always calls to mind the work of Vermeer and the careful delineations of the complex shapes are masterful exercises in perspective. This painting probably dates from some time after 1650 and is signed (EVARISTVS BASCHENIS F.). It was given to the Musées Royaux in 1908.

· 19 ·

SALVATOR ROSA
(1615-1673)

The Temptation of St. Anthony

Canvas, 49¼″ x 36.5″
Palazzo Pitti, Florence

In her classic biography of Salvator Rosa, published in 1824, Lady Sidney Morgan admitted to being more attracted by the artist's life than his art. It was Rosa's "qualities of an Italian patriot, who, stepping boldly in advance of a degraded age, stood in the foreground of his times . . . when all around him was timid mannerism and grovelling subserviency," that excited her admiration. Certainly Rosa was a restless, many-sided individual whose sojourns in Florence and Rome as well as his native Naples gave him ample opportunity to exercise his gifts for social satire in plays and poetry. But his position as an artist was far from negligible. His wildly romantic landscapes caught the imagination of his contemporaries and even later generations to such an extent that the mere mention of his name was enough to call up visions of wild, dangerous, woodlands or perilous mountain passes.

Even in his few religious works, this wild and turbulent atmosphere persists. The *Temptation of St. Anthony* was done, according to Rosa's biographer Baldinucci, for Cardinal Gian Carlo de Medici. The Saint seizes the cross to defend himself from the monstrous apparitions. There is a threatening, disturbing overtone to much of Rosa's art which had an enormous appeal to the early nineteenth century Romantics.

· 20 ·

GIOVANNI BATTISTA
GAULLI
called "BACICCIO"
or "BACICCIA"
(1639-1709)

*The Adoration of
the Name of Jesus*

Fresco and sculpture
Gesù, Rome

Between 1672 and 1683 Gaulli undertook the transformation of the interior of the Gesù, the principal church of the Society of Jesus. His decorations in the semi-dome of the apse, the cupola, the pendentives, the vault of the nave and the vault of the chapel of St. Ignatius heralded a new era, in Roman church decoration. The ceiling of the nave, representing *The Adoration of the Name of Jesus,* was unveiled in 1679. Architecture, sculpture, and fresco painting were fused together in such a way that it is almost impossible to tell where one ends and the other begins. By painting on flaps which actually projected over the architecture, Gaulli created an ensemble in which the tangible world and the mystic vision have become inextricably united. At the apex of the fresco are the symbolic letters of Christ's name: I.H.S., surmounted by a cross. They give forth a dazzling burst of light which appears to illuminate the whole composition. From the darkness below, our eyes are drawn upward toward the radiant climax. All of the component parts have been welded together in subordination to the almost overpowering all-over effect.

Gaulli had been one of Bernini's most talented collaborators and was strongly influenced by his artistic thinking. The Gesù decorations are a monumental elaboration of Bernini's daring experiment in the Cornaro Chapel in S. Maria della Vittoria (See color slide 13). Gaulli's work set the pattern for Roman church decoration during the next decades. Its influence was enormous and can be seen not only throughout Italy but also in Germany and Austria.

· 21 ·

GIOVANNI BENEDETTO
CASTIGLIONE
called "IL GRECHETTO"
(ca. 1610-1665)

The Crucifixion

Paper pasted on canvas,
25⅛″ x 21⅝″
Palazzo Bianco, Genoa

Castiglione is the most important figure of the mid-century Genoese school of painting, though in the course of his career he was also active in Rome, Naples, Venice, and Mantua where he was appointed court painter in 1648. A distinguished draughtsman, he was also a fine print maker and is credited with the invention of the monotype, a single-proof printing process in which the artist paints directly on the copper plate. He seems to have been able to profitably absorb most of the artistic currents of his time and owes a good deal to Bernini and Poussin as well as Rubens and Rembrandt.

The *Crucifixion,* painted during the latter part of the artist's life is an extraordinary picture by any standard. The dazzling virtuosity and boldness of execution that is Castiglione's hallmark is seen at its best in his smaller works such as this. His intensely personal "Grand Manner" had an important influence on his contemporaries as well as on the Genoese painters whose activities belong more to the eighteenth century.

· 22 ·

CARLO MARATTI
(1625-1713)

*The Virgin Appearing to
St. Philip Neri*

Canvas, 135″ x 77½″
Palazzo Pitti, Florence

Not long before 1674 Maratti was commissioned by a Florentine Senator, Pietro Nerli, to execute this painting for the Roman church of S. Giovanni dei Fiorentini. It was taken to Florence later by Prince Ferdinando de' Medici and replaced in the church by a copy.

No artist better exemplifies the artistic taste of late seventeenth century Rome than Carlo Maratti. Long before he died he was considered the foremost painter of his age and his manner was enormously influential. Maratti's links are with the classicizing artists of the earlier part of the century, particularly with Andrea Sacchi under whom he had been trained. Both his color scheme and his idealization of types—to the point where individual peculiarities have been abandoned in favor of generalized representations in accord with a predetermined standard of beauty—set him off from his immediate predecessors in the Baroque camp such as Gaulli. Maratti's work had the full approval of the most influential critics of the age, among them Giovanni Pietro Bellori whose *Idea of Beauty*, first delivered as an address at the Roman Academy of St. Luke in 1642, set the tone of critical judgments throughout the seventeenth and much of the eighteenth century. Not only were Bellori and Marratti close friends but Bellori prepared a biography of the artist and also of Maratti's teacher, Sacchi, which was to have formed the second part of a series called "Lives of the Artists" of which the first part included the biographies of Annibale Carracci, Domenichino and Poussin but not—and this is revealing—Bernini.

Maratti's work is that of an artist in complete command of his repertory. He continued to produce his altarpieces, portraits and representations of the Madonna and Child with the confident assurance of an artist who had no doubts about the direction of his talents. Maratti's "Grand Manner" was to become almost international, influencing artists until the beginning of the Romantic movement.

· 23 ·

LUCA GIORDANO
(1632-1705)

St. Francis Xavier Baptizing the Neophytes and St. Francis Borgia

Canvas, 165¾″ x 124″
Capodimonte, Naples

More than any other artist, the Neapolitan painter Luca Giordano can be credited with spreading the Roman "Grand Manner" throughout Europe. His activity touched the most important art centers of the day, Rome, Venice, and Florence and for ten years (1692-1702) he served as court painter in Madrid. The speed with which he worked astonished his contemporaries. This enormous painting, formerly in the church of San Francesco Saverio in Naples, is said to have been executed in only three days!

Giordano had an astonishing ability to assimilate the manner of other painters, and the influences of artists from Dürer to Rembrandt and Raphael to Annibale Carracci can be seen in his work. His thorough familiarity with the entire historic tradition of European painting and his willingness to adopt whatever served his purpose mark the beginning of a new era in Italian painting. He is the predecessor of the "international" Italian artists of the eighteenth century who served in courts from St. Petersburg to Madrid.

· 24 ·

FRANCESCO SOLIMENA
(1657-1747)

The Rape of Orithyia

Canvas, 39¾″ x 54⅛″
Palazzo Spada, Rome

Neapolitan painting of the late seventeenth and early eighteenth centuries is completely dominated by the towering figure of Francesco Solimena. Though he spent most of his working life in Naples, his reputation was truly international and his pupils ranged from Rome to Madrid. Neapolitan churches are still filled with his altarpieces and frescoes but some of Solimena's finest works were the small scale mythologies which he executed for private patrons. *The Rape of Orithyia* illustrates Ovid's tale of Boreas, the personification of the north wind, who carried off Orithyia, daughter of the King of Athens. It was painted in 1700 for Cardinal Fabrizio Spada Veralli during a short trip which Solimena made to Rome.

It was from the masters of the Roman Baroque, Lanfranco and Pietro da Cortona, as well as from Luca Giordano, that Solimena drew his inspiration. but his artistic repertory was wide enough to include poses and figures borrowed from the Carracci as well as from Raphael. Like Luca Giordano, he was fully acquainted with the whole tradition of Italian art and picked and chose what he felt could be useful to him. Solimena's domination of the Italian scene is the concluding chapter of seventeenth century Italian painting and from Naples at the end of the seventeenth century, the center of emphasis shifted to Venice and the work of Tiepolo during the eighteenth.